Praise for When She Was Bad

Lust. Love. Betrayal and loyalty. Temptation and hilarity. Gabrielle Freeman dissects her speakers' hearts, tenderly, with supreme attention to what it is to be human, female, and fierce. Gabrielle Freeman's poems are bad—by which I mean badass bold. Michael Jackson bad. Freeman's bad and you know it. That's why you read her. *When She Was Bad* is a smart, compassionate, tightly crafted and explosive debut.
— Denise Duhamel, author of *SCALD*

The poems of Gabrielle Freeman's *When She Was Bad* are by turns amorous, witty, fierce, ironic and erudite, but they are always sensual and often erotic. As the title suggests, Freeman explores the promises and surprises of the human heart, and her deft free verse addresses temptations, rewards and disappointments. Her bold inquiries sharpen both her eye and her tongue, but her first collection is far from single-minded, as she makes room for owls, spider wort, Bela Lugosi, Stephen King, Kareem Abdul-Jabbar and Renoir. *When She Was Bad* is entertaining and enlightening, and with its publication Gabrielle Freeman steps onto the stage in full voice, singing true.
—R.T. Smith, editor of *Shenandoah* and author of
In the Night Orchard: New and Selected Poems

Gabrielle Freeman's *When She Was Bad* is about passion: sex, love, loss, life at its most elemental. One poem challenges, "Did you bare your neck or your teeth?" These poems bare neck and teeth. They are fierce and tender, and each poem so full of energy that the page can barely contain it.
—Suzanne Cleary, author of *Beauty Mark*

Gabrielle Freeman's poetry is fecund, sensuous, and refreshing. I admire the *strangeness* in these poems—not a strangeness of obliquity or constructed befuddlement, but an unpredictability that ultimately clarifies, inducing *empathy*. In her poems I can hear "on the morning road . . . the cello's throat" as it "opens into a blur of birds and fog." Her poems transcend delicate transcription of events; instead, they entice and enrich, offer room for a reader's imagination to blossom with interpretation. These are pieces by a soul who understands the importance of the world behind the world, a place to which few gain access.
—William Wright, series editor of *The Southern Poetry Anthology*, and author of *Tree Heresies*

This may be a first collection, but it doesn't feel like it. In a book filled with the brilliant observations of an amazing eye and mind, Gabrielle Freeman is thoroughly in command of her poetic instrument. The sensuousness and frank eroticism of these poems hold the attention of even the most easily distracted reader and keep us turning pages, as in a good novel. This is a book you are going to want to own.
—Richard Tillinghast, author of *An Armchair Traveller's History of Istanbul: City of Remembering and Forgetting*

When She Was Bad

When She Was Bad

Poems

Gabrielle Brant Freeman

Press 53
Winston-Salem

Press 53, LLC
PO Box 30314
Winston-Salem, NC 27130

First Edition

Copyright © 2016 by Gabrielle Brant Freeman

All rights reserved, including the right of reproduction in whole or in part in any form except in the case of brief quotations embodied in critical articles or reviews. For permission, contact publisher at editor@Press53.com, or at the address above.

Cover design by Dawn D. Surratt

Cover images, Copyright © 2016 by Dawn D. Surratt,
used by permission of the artist.
www.dawndhanna.com

Author photo by Dawn D. Surratt

Printed on acid-free paper
ISBN 978-1-941209-47-9

For Lynn Gay Beaulieu Smith

Acknowledgments

The author thanks the editors of the publications where the following poems first appeared:

Barrelhouse, "All the Things We Have in Common"

Clockhouse Review, "Cross Streets"

Cider Press Review, "Your Mask Is a Gift"

Eunoia Review, "Want" and "Wanted"

Gabby, "The Happily Married Woman Boards the Plane"

Grist, "How Things Build: On Botticelli's *Primavera*"

Hobart, "In all the months that end" and "*Keep your shirt on*"

HocTok, "On Renoir's *Odalisque*" and "To Go Without"

Melancholy Hyperbole, "The Sorrowful Lover Stands"

Minetta Review, "The Art of Deception"

MiPOesias, "Bite Down, Hard"

Rappahannock Review, "Back Seat Event"

storySouth, "Failure to Obliterate"

Waxwing, "Your Own Lecherous Heart"

"Aubade" was chosen for the Norton Center's 2016 exhibit titled "EAT: A Literature and Photography Installation."

"Failure to Obliterate" won the 2015 Randall Jarrell Poetry Competition sponsored by the North Carolina Writers' Network.

"Laying Claim" was a semi-finalist in the 2015 James Applewhite Poetry Competition sponsored by the *North Carolina Literary Review*.

Contents

Keep your shirt on,	1
Back Seat Event	2
Bite Down, Hard	3
The Audacious Canvas	5
On Renoir's *Odalisque*	7
When She Was Bad	8
Failure to Obliterate	9
To Go Without	10
Laying Claim	11
Resistance. Attraction.	13
Aubade	14
Still Life	16
To Make Love	17
Whore	18
The Art of Deception	20
One of these statements is true	22
Your Own Lecherous Heart	23
Wanted	24
Since you weren't using it,	25
Want	26
Selling the House	27
The Sorrowful Lover Stands	29
How to Snag a Man	30
Geography	32
Poem Automatic	33
Recollections	34
3-5 Days without Water	35
Listening to Hendrix on vinyl, eating breakfast, and thinking of your hands	36
Dear Valentine,	37
Your Mask Is a Gift	38
Love with No Apparent Function	40
Devenir Chêvre	41
Sex with a Novelist	42

The Happily Married Woman Boards the Plane	43
T & A	44
Glamour Church	46
Mooning	47
Pedestal	48
Murmuration	49
All the Things We Have in Common	50
How Things Build: On Botticelli's *Primavera*	51
Cross Streets	52
In all the months that end	55

Keep your shirt on,

                                        she says,
and I know she means wait,
be patient, calm down,
but I can't help but think
about what would happen
if I took my shirt off.

Certainly the room would not
darken with bodies clutched
in a tight ring around us,
sweat beading up on foreheads
creased in anticipation,
backs tensed, fists clenched
around crumpled, damp dollars.

A heated unbuttoning
of the button-down,
a shrugging out of creased sleeves.
Weak light from a bare bulb swinging
from an industrial ceiling,
conduits and pipes gleaming dull
and dripping. Not the promise
of connecting flesh,
bare knuckles and tender ribs.

Not the possible toss
to the concrete, knees pressed
to shoulders, thighs flexed,
straining tailored fabric.
Not an undulant roar,
a chanting pant of mob,
breathless for the bruise,
desperate for the thick, wet smack.

I finger the fine bone,
the line of white buttons down
to my cut-weight waist.

Back Seat Event

I.

I want to kiss you, but
I open the car door, and it is raining.
I know the cloth seat will only keep our heat
for the amount of time it takes to unfold into the wet night
and you behind me.
Your lips are not warm and flushed on the back of my neck.
Your lips are not pressed to my open palms.
Your lips are not gently insistent,
nor are they stripped back. In open moan.

II.

On the morning road, the cello's throat opens
into a blur of birds and fog. I know
there are too many birds to divine.
Deliberate deep draw of the bow
and a single crow is caught
backward in thick mist, bourbon slow.
Loosed mercy. My feathered hands
press denim, measure the heat
of my breath against cold glass.

III.

I dream of birds. I'm saying
I know steel, glass stand between me, mist,
and rain. I'm saying I know there are
too many birds to count.
Your lips are a low note drawn
slow across burnished cello hips,
fingers insistent on strings. The heat
of your moan stripped bare on the pane.
I trace it. I beg you.

Bite Down, Hard

The valet folds into your '67 Bug,
pressed pants snag on cracked upholstery.
He grinds the clutch and bucks around the curve
of the wooded Hollywood Hills drive.

Bela Lugosi's old house is cloistered,
haloed by party glow in the back.
We penetrate the heavy front door,
pass the powder room swathed in crimson damask.

Tour the kitchen, brick hearth, hand-painted
Mexican tile. Lugosi's private bath,
gold-plated fixtures on porcelain bidet,
urinal, toilet. On the burgundy walls,

framed black-and-white hermaphrodite nudes,
art prints, figures posed like Botticelli's
Venus in the desert. Skeleton trees,
fire-blackened, vie with lush hair, breasts, cocks.

The birthday party is in the back. Tasteful
arrangements adorn tables set with silver,
crystal. The Grecian pool shimmers Tiffany
blue. Rich classmates' exfoliated faces

kiss our cheeks. Silk stockings whisper against
understated charcoal shantung, rub
against tailored slacks. Your ironed khakis,
my nearly one-paycheck, black, crushed-velvet dress

compel us to drink what is offered,
smoke what is offered. Bite down hard
on our unsuitable awkwardness,
on the stiff bit of our abrupt discontent.

Our only recourse is to stake claim.
Beneath the beatific hermaphrodites'
smiles, I sink my teeth into your pliant
flesh. You push your stiffening body

into mine, a furnace. Crimson flames crackle
your ebony hair, a mass of fuses.
We are all that we possess. Amid smoke
and languid ash, blood blooms our cheeks.

You fight the clutch down the hill, LA
laid out below us like a painted whore
in a well-lit room, her loosened corset
our native soil, well-suited for sleep.

The Audacious Canvas

The Lucian Freud paintings at the MOMA
in 2005 arrested me from around
a corner artificially made
for just such effect. The breasts like white
watermelons, flesh stretched beyond
the capacity of comprehension.
Bellies slack in sleep on couches, reclined
in regular chairs like no one would ever sit
at home but for those who make a study
of themselves. Have you ever rested, spread-eagle
naked on your La-Z-Boy watching *Big Bang Theory*
or *Chopped*? Maybe it's just me, but even
all alone, kids and husband out of town,
I wear my most comfortable clothes, threadbare
but covering flesh I might pinch or grasp
in both hands and jiggle like my diabetic
grandfather attempting to terrorize
his grandchildren. "Cm'ere, girlie," he'd leer,
pull up his tobacco stained t-shirt, jab
his fat with the orange-tipped syringe. Shake
the significant segment of skin,
navel like a blind eye, the plastic plunger
shimmying in grotesque display.

Freud's nudes demand attention in their natural-ness,
the anti-selfie, the true portrayal
of the body. The flaccid penis,
the diminutive buttocks topped with a torso
like a bloated carcass three days
on the side of the road. I don't mean
to denigrate. The body is the body
is the body. Freud's *Kate Moss* is as likely
to make me want to avert my eyes
as *Benefits Supervisor Sleeping*.
You should see them!

Maybe it's that I am just as fucking convinced
of my own body's shortcomings, of my own fat
deposits, ill-conceived imperfections, as the next girl
grown on lingerie catalogues and swim suit
models, soft-focus lighting and Spanx.

If I knew an artist like Freud,
I would beg to pose, skin loose in repose,
not arranged like poppies in a vase of blue glass
on a Moroccan table inlaid,
but a woman whose beauty lies in her eyes,
closed against the end of the long work day.
Whose body is a study in color,
hollow, shadow, and bulge. I would see this shell
as it is, and I, too, would gape.
Stand before the audacious canvas and stare.

On Renoir's *Odalisque*

You see what you want.
Full vase on a decadent pouf, foreign
oranges. Full vase shod in feathered mules,
draped head to shin. The allure
of calf and turn of ankle, the gentle
fold of neck. The thin white strip
of teeth lined in striking pink, thin
brown strip of iris lined in kohl.
Bloom and flame. What you want
is Odalisque, parted lips, parted legs,
looking straight at you through hooded
eyes. Thick brown braid, flamboyant
headdress, oversized earrings dripping
gold. Everything other, sensuous difference.
Beneath the silk sash, the sheer blouse,
the brocade harem pants, you envision
virginal skin. A most delicate bondage,
this *objet d'art*, deliberately stroked,
gilt framed. Nailed to the wall.

When She Was Bad

What does having a curl
*right in the middle
of her forehead* have to do
with anything? This little girl,
her attitudinal dichotomy.
Very, very good or
horrid. The curl, coquettish,
belying innocence.

Is that what this is all about?
Can she only be
very, very good, or
a rosy cheeked Lilith,
dimpled demon?

Her clear-eyed knowing:
trouble.

Failure to Obliterate

Beneath the storm stippled surface, the manta ray's great gills flex,
the iron grate of a furnace venting.
Flames lick and chew.

Beneath the scarred skin at my throat, uneven excision
of my body's failure to obliterate vestigial gills.
Three scars pull me from the sea into this rain.

The ray is a cabernet on the tongue after rare beef blood.
Fat suspended in juices like brief rings of light dripping off the chin
on to the breast.

The ray is the last breadth of a minor chord,
vibration of taut strings. Sound takes the shape of the body
like smoke in a glass.

The ray is the thrum of adrenalin, the enamel-smooth shaft
of a sabertooth canine. Run a fingertip down its length.
Pierce ancient flesh. Rip it out in pulsing chunks.
Brace back feet, embrace the corded neck, latch on
to the muscled shoulder.

Beneath the surface, the ray swims, its mouth open, full
with salt and the hum of skin. I fill my mouth
with deep red notes of tobacco and black pepper.
The salt crown of want, of subtle, of sweet.

The ray considers the sound of rain on the water's surface.
It sounds like every other water. It does not
dilute. It slips over the ray's gray skin, over the thick slits.
It breaks on the ray's bloody gills.

I want the deep back.
I want the deep fire to draw me into its open mouth,
to tongue my skin, to drip blood and fat. To expose me an instrument.
I want to be undone.

To Go Without

(Italicized lines from Gluck's "Che Faro Senza Euridice?")

Breasts taped down tight, she dresses for her role;
creased black trousers, charcoal button-down, hair
slicked back in a tight plait. This Orfeo
will weep.

Euridice! Euridice!

Libretto of two lovers, one snake-bit,
slight pinch of the needle, hot blood courses,
spins to the underworld, forsythia
wound in her dark curls.

Oh Dio! Rispondi!

Voice lifted in lament, Orfeo defies
tradition, follows her one-day wife down.
Euridice, specter, all sweat and ice
beneath the ruined lace.

Rispondi!

Delicate petals seamed gray in their crush.
Orfeo kneels in Elysium. Unbraids her hair.

Laying Claim

In the local history room, we pretend
it's an accident when our fingers touch
as we pore over texts, pretend your thigh
isn't pressed up against mine beneath the desk.

We find a legend. There is always
a legend like this: lovers destined
to be separate, their rash act, the permanent
curse reminder. They become a strong wind
to whip wet cheeks, a perfect furl of bloom
on a gnarled tree, impossible pillars of stone.

This is Cherokee country. Winter-bare trees reveal
leaf-packed forest floors. Worn paths wind
down to Green River, a flat-rock promise
of a summer swim, of wading,
soft moss beneath bare feet. Falling filtered light.

We find that five hundred years ago, a chief
gave provisions to deSoto and his men,
to the Christians. *Slaves, corn, and little dogs,
probably opossums.* DeSoto derives
from thicket or grove, trees standing close
to water, trees surrounding a clearing
where families gathered, ate the white flesh
of fish caught in the Pacolet,
tanned hides, met these strangers with pearls.
DeSoto's men rested their horses. Searched for gold.

You say, "Everybody claims deSoto,"
slide the length of your long body away
slow. I flatten yellowed, cracking newsprint.

There is always a legend like this.
A woman waits in a clearing
at the edge of the woods, the greening rim

of a thicket of pine, the thick slope
of the Green River, the dappled edge
of the Pacolet. Pyrite shimmer
flows through the winter-bare trees on a warm wind
like dust caught in an early morning ray
through a window. Her lover joins her.
Words stretch tight, catch in their throats like pearls,
like tiny bones. The wind picks up, presses
them together like paper. The gods
would turn them into a flowering tree,
to stone. Her lover lifts her hair, spreads
his fingers through its light like thin gold veins.

Resistance. Attraction.

The rising sun stirs the gray in your hair.
Somewhere, animals wake and muster
in their shelters, preen feathers and stretch
night-dull muscles, but we are in the house
of our mutual resistance having
little talks in words like running a thumb
across parted lips, like the first taste of scotch
from the bottle. Every public moment
a big parade, everyone in step, painted
big smiles and marching, marching. We are still.
Don't wake me up. I am not sleeping.

Here you are with sun dawning in your hair.
We've been up all night in the house of our
mutual attraction having little talks
like water in a clear glass. I would run
fingers though my hair, stretch my body
in rising light. Hit you right between the eyes.

Aubade

There is strong coffee in the morning
and a bicycle I ride into the little town
to pick up the lemon-almond twist you covet
like sneaking a fingertip into buttercream
piped at the back of a cake. The pastry
is softly layered and flakes into the napkin
in your lap. You sit cross-legged on top
of the down comforter pulled loose into place
so stray crumbs won't get tangled in the sheets.
I watch the sun contour your morning face.

There are eclectic storefronts, and we wander
into a street market where we sample cheeses
and chocolates. I watch your mouth as we taste.
Sweet tang of grass. Deep, earthy melt.

There is a shore, and I stand at the edge,
my feet sinking deeper with each rush,
as you dive beneath the farthest breaker.
I watch the water make an island of your body.

There is a counter dusted with flour.
We stand side-by-side, turn out the dough,
punch it down. Brief rise of yeast. I watch
as your strong hands press and turn.

There is a gentle breeze coming over the water.
I smell the ocean drying in your hair.

There is wine. I watch you trace the flight of bats
with your palms through deep blue purpling black.

There are stars and stars. Your skin's night luster.

I feel the advent of the sun on this, our first almost
morning. You see, we've only just met, and we've spent hours
talking under someone else's strings of party lights.
I have watched a perfect day conceived between us.

I kiss you because I want to. I kiss you
to block your view of the brief orange glow
on the horizon, to keep you here for just another little while
before we both must go.

Still Life

sketch it out like you want it.
circle table, circle plate,
triangle toast, butter square,
cylinder mug, rectangle book
canted to the plate. ink it.
quick strokes overlap,
cross-hatch. squiggle butter melt.
add a parabolic banana.
wash in the background.
blue tipped with orange early morning.
loose green mist of trees.
add tall glass with ice.
pass color block over breakfast.
ink black wrought iron, fern green
plate, mustard golden toast,
cadmium yellow butter,
antique white souvenir mug,
saddle brown coffee,
mustard golden tea.
press in, blend out with fingertips.
wash in light.
outline a state on the mug.
title the book.
stroke charcoal quick along ink lines and pull
to fade, broad strokes and pull
edges to ashes.

this is morning like you want it. still life.
it is implied that we are in the room
just off the deck. I am keeping you
from your toast. you are keeping me
from my coffee.
let them cool.

To Make Love

Take an old, white undershirt
finally retired to an oil rag
in the garage, soft as the skin
of your sun-browned belly
when you were young. Rip it open
with teasing teeth, lay it wide.
Upend the ribbed tin can filled
with the rusted remains
of leftover bolts, bent nails.
Finger the silt of corrosion,
the sift and fall of heat,
of moisture. Nuts small, smooth,
slick grease and silver shine;
thick and heavy in the palm
like a breast cupped just
as the last slip of sleep slides down
slow. Press the blush of rust
into the worn cotton, thumb
into persistent stains of work
and sweat. Fill the cloth hollow
with the bite of pointed screws,
thin strips of threads sharp,
stripped down bare by rough fingers,
repeated push and drive
of calloused hands.

Gather the fabric by its jagged edges.
Cinch shut tight with a slip of jute twine,
worn, frayed, and firm.

Whore

I didn't know then how to respond when Jen confessed,
"I fucked a guy in the bathroom last night at my work party."
She cleared her throat right before she spoke. I said, "Um."
I should have asked about logistics. Was he sitting
on the toilet? Did her knees rub salmon metal walls?
Did her hands grip the pipes for leverage? Was she standing,
bent at the hips, hands splayed on cool tile? His ass inches
from the door, her skirt bunched up in his fists?
Perhaps there was no stall. Perhaps it was a stand-alone
toilet. Perhaps he lifted her by the backs of robust thighs,
drunk-strong, forearms roping with each thrust, the zipper
on her dress catching splintered wood on the locked door,
his pants around his ankles, his trim silver belt buckle
clanking time like the slap of a flagpole halyard in the wind.

I'll never be able to hear the slap of a flagpole halyard again
without thinking about furtive sex in bathrooms.
And every time I eat at a restaurant with long tablecloths,
I think about Anna who blew her date beneath one
while we all sat there pretending it wasn't happening.
It's hard to eat your grilled chicken Caesar while the guy
next to you in the tufted leather booth is being fluffed
and finished, his mouth open like a fish and making small
gasping noises. Anna reappeared, and I couldn't stop
looking at her lips. In a movie, all sound would slow down,
slur while the camera focused on her mouth, lipstick worn off
to the liner, forming words. There would be comic timing
and laughter in the theater at her audacity, at his
pleased discomfort, trying to keep a straight face.

I'm no good at keeping a straight face, not when asked
if I ever want to go back to being twenty
again and be a bigger whore than I was.
Meghan and Holly waited for my answer, sipping
mimosas out of plastic football-shaped glasses.
I had a vision of Meghan kneeling on the floor
of a cottage, a prick in each hand, more watching.
Her legendary penchant for exhibition.

I said, "Um." Because I wasn't. A whore. Of course, I suppose
that depends on your definition of whore. Is it when,
at seventeen, you let beer-soaked recruits fresh
from basic training slide their hands over your breasts
in Tijuana where the music is so loud and the dance floor
is so tight you kiss a stranger's ear to be heard?

In TJ, it's impossible not to be pressed up tight
against a couple of someones. It's so hot, and beer,
tequila, and sweat make you slippery and loose.
Lights flash and strobe so that even when your eyes
are open, you can't see. When you feel fingers
slip-slide under the hem of your slinky shirt,
you're not sure whose they are. And, really. Who cares?
Are you a whore when, once a year, every year, you
meet your lover at a retreat, fuck each other raw
until it's time to go home to your family? Your two
beautiful children? When people at the retreat whisper
about you and your lover, they say "star-crossed" and "meant for."
They imagine every twist of white cotton hotel sheet,
every steam-filled, hot hotel shower, every single

tiny bar of soap lathered, applied. Hot hotel showers
are good places to think about whether you would
go back and do it over, answer yes when you said no.
About the etymology of whore, which turns out
to be anything from *girl, lass, wench* to *one who desires*
to *adulterer* to *she-wolf* to *publicly exposed*
to *bitch* to *foreskin of a horse's penis*. I'm not sure which
Meghan and Holly meant, although I'm positive
it wasn't the latter. But she-wolf has appeal. I should
have said, No, not a whore. Not a woman doing someone else's
version of wrong. But a *lupa*, maybe. A *sexually voracious female*.
Prowl. Stalk. Hunt. Moonlit howling power.

When Jen told me she fucked a guy in the bathroom, I should
have asked, did you like it? Did you bare your neck or your teeth?

19

The Art of Deception

If I knew how you liked your eggs—scrambled,
over-medium, poached, over-easy—
I've since forgotten. That, and your coffee.
Black? And whether you took sugar or honey
in your tea, or whether you drank tea. Fragile,
memory. I feel the smooth blue shell

found when I was six, but not the warm shell
left by your nightly body, scrambled
into nylon PT shorts, sun fragile
breaking into dawn. Funny how easy
it is to forget the taste of your honey-
gold skin, but not the taste of café

au lait in New Orleans, beignets browned,
dusted. To forget the sound of your seashell
voice, lips to my ear, whispering honey,
but not the sound of crawfish scrambling
in a plastic bucket. To forget the ease
of your lies, the ease with which my fragile

heart shattered, but not the fragility
of a nest beneath my window, coffee-
colored twigs cradling tiny eggs. I eased
it into a box, hung it so its shells,
baby blue, would not be threatened by scrambling
snakes. You swallowed me whole. Words, honey

from your mouth. I should have known the honeymoon
was over, but I hate feeling fragile,
and so I believed you when you scrambled
your stories. The kid at the coffee-shop
knew, for Christ's sake. You were just a shell,
hollow, an aching need. I made it easy

for you to seem whole. It isn't easy
to admit being fooled, duped by a phoney
like you. Afterwards, I would shellac
my confidence on when I was more fragile
than glass. Every morning, I made coffee,
sweet, just for me. Just for me, eggs, scrambled.

I could lie and make it easy: scrambled.
But I've forgotten, dissolved like honey in coffee.
I make feathers of eggshells beneath my fragile feet.

One of these statements is true

Your eyes are the milky blue of an uncertain winter morning.
Once, you looked into me and saw something you wanted.
At no point were you ever out of control.
Your eyes are gunmetal gray when you are angry.
I never dream about the smell of the ocean on your skin.
Once, you brought home a nice bottle of wine just because.
I had no doubts as I walked towards you in my mother's veil.
Your eyes, the color of every tropical shore, never gave you away.
At no point did I ever think about how someone else's hands would feel.
I never saw it coming.

Your Own Lecherous Heart

(title from *Dives and Pauper*, Anonymous)

I imagine you cruising the boulevard at two a.m.
in your dead mother's car, watching the girls
sway out of the bars, hands resting on the soft curves
of their girlfriends' waists, mouths open and laughing, your view
of the tops of their breasts and pink push-up bras enhanced
by their mirth. They are bending for you. Long, tanned legs
engender a gentle swing of skirt. Their hair begs
to be touched. Dick in hand, you quiver at each glance.

Their brightly colored faces trail like sparklers
on a hot night, lithe bodies leave a primordial
scent of amber and cloves. Their eyes, their skin, fire
only for you. You believe everything is yours,
and you take it. Pink and pliant, your mouth, your tongue
like flayed salmon, gills flushed with blood. Your long fingers,
your sex deep within body after body. Their flesh sings
for you. Naked, you drive and watch, drive and hunt.

The hole inside you is deep and black. I imagine
blue lights strobing, the officer's face as you roll down
the window, dilate into that bright light, a hint of frown
furrowed between your clear eyes, your wide sheepish grin.
As you confess, I imagine your skin lit up blue
like lividity, your body dead as the soul
you keep trying to revive, paying the ferryman toll
after toll in skin, but still drowning.

Wanted

Time to squander, enough to study owls
in their nightly hunt, eyes wide, talons flashing,
scooping cicadas and mice from purpling
grass, leaving neat packages of hair and bone.

How, like the owl, you watched me, dared me frolic
for a moment under the moon, craters
plain on its face, lava's heat long forgotten,
reflected in the icy limestone circle

Floridian spring. I dared play, gambol,
dive breathless, flip my mercurial tail,
emerge into silken night, dripping stars.
You struck. Absconded with my insides, soft

parts. Left a cage, bilious shell, elusive
heart. Beats echo in me from wherever you are.

Since you weren't using it,

I swam in your pool last Tuesday morning.
Your blue foam floaty with the head pillow
is perfect for watching thin clouds creep
across the silver sky like dust bunnies
when someone quick opens a door. They tumble.
And since you weren't using it, I let myself in
and walked around your house in the deep
brown leather slippers with top stitching
and sheepskin that you always set neatly
next to your side of the bed with the toes pointed
out so you can slip into them at three
in the morning when you wake up to wander
and draw water. They are so soft
and they make a satisfying shuffle
over your chocolate walnut floors like
rubbing dry flesh with the palm. Since
you weren't using it, I poured a glass
of your good chardonnay into the stemless
glass you carry with you to bed and wash
and set to dry each morning before you make
the coffee. Your bed is firm and full
with lavender and coconut. Your detergent,
your shampoo. You weren't using it,
but I put everything back exactly,
since it was time for you to come home.

Want

The portable turntable still plays.
Just so you know. I got it out last night,
sat on the deck with a stack of our records,
the bottle of good scotch we were saving.

The needle still works, but the speed
isn't quite right, and the records are scratched,
so all the songs go in and out like some
'60s hippy dancer pop-art montage,

hands waving, expounding on an hourglass,
broken up by an occasional
bad film splice. A flash of nothing,
then a figure, pulled into action

like a marionette. Long skirts swirling;
ugly headbands. That signature vinyl
sound: anticipation. Put the needle
on the record. Hold your breath. The stars

only clarified that you are traveling,
like some latter-day effing wise man
run off with your gold and your myrrh,
looking to present to someone who isn't

me. It didn't work, the scotch. I dreamed
I woke up, saw you strap your shoes on,
light a cigarette, the way you do
on the bench at the foot of our bed.

I watched you from behind, cupping your hand
around the flame. And then I woke up
expecting to see you there, smell your night sweat
and hand-rolled tobacco. But the bench remains

empty. The bottle and the street,
they comfort me. I wear them like smoke.

Selling the House

It's been hard to get used to, the glut of green,
cunning kudzu climbing, mounded moss spattered
on brick, feelers loosening mortar, lichen on granite
like teeming flakes of paint. To get used to mosquitoes
lighting on legs bared to the sun, bugs numerous as rice
in a new bride's bin, always full for luck. Bites bloom.

Spotted lilies in stagnant ditches, bright blooms
arching open to meet the light. Waist-high stalks green
as jade you cannot buy for yourself. The price
of fortune. Crepe myrtles' smooth trunks, branches spotted
with pink. Pools of shade teeming with mosquitoes.
They say only the females bite. I took for granted

my anger would remain hidden, dark granite
buried deep. This house. Our house. The irises bloomed
first. I waited for them in early spring, before mosquitoes
rose from damp. Leaves like slim blades greening.
No matter. It's been hard to fathom the spatter
of spider wort, white-throated honeysuckle, the caprice

with which you left me. I had hardly brushed my hair free of rice,
removed the coin from my shoe. I ate the pomegranate.
Thought you'd stay forever. You moved me, promise of patter
of little feet. I traded home for you, sand for bloom,
concrete and asphalt for corridors of thrumming green.
I share my morning coffee with mosquitoes.

I wonder if the blood from the broken mosquito
smeared on my shoulder is yours. Small sacrifice.
I sit among brown boxes, stare out at the green.
My anger rises. It pushes up like granite
bursts from burgeoning earth, like fire blooms
in the desert, tinder sends sparks into dark spatter

of stars. I wish that every single thing you touch sputters
and dies. I call the gods for a plague of mosquitoes,

for crusting, puss-filled multitudes of blooms
to visit your tender skin. I see maggot-riddled rice
in your new kitchen, irreparable cracks in your granite
countertops, unending encroachment of mold the exact green

of my eyes. May it spatter your drywall like rice
thrown at our feet. May you be buried toes facing west, granted
nothing but the memory of my body's bloom when I was young

and green.

The Sorrowful Lover Stands

a table is set in the middle of an image
of the high plains. clouds white and clouds purpling
sit at the wide horizon. low roll of timpani.
the table is covered in white billowing

in wind caught like the hem of a dress caught
like hair unpinned. there are grasses in hummocks
clear to the heavy sky. on the table
a heavy candelabra black weighs down

the shroud white like a sail like a crisp
button-down come untucked and stuck in time.
a page turned between movements. a cough.
there is a gash in the earth at the bottom

of the image a crack zagging toward the table
scouring the grasses. a simple case of the earth
opening up and swallowing. I stand
in front of the image. my hair loose caught

in a scouring wind. the hem of my dress billows
behind me. the fabric traces my topography
rolling landscape of blue silk. I am caught
at the top of a breath my chest high.

there is no one at the table in the image
stark against the blue sky at the top.
clear soaring soprano. I stand outside
the image in silence like a gash.

I cannot reach the table and there are no chairs
on which to sit. my mouth is wide
at the top of a breath and the note is caught
in heavy quiet. I cannot make a sound.

How to Snag a Man

Snag is one of those words, isn't it?
Those words that start to look ridiculous
the more you write them. Snag, snag, snag,
snag, snag, snag, snag, snag, snag. Snag.

It starts to twist into nsag, into gans.
You start to wonder if that's how it's really spelled.
And then you can't remember, can't trust
your rusty brain. You go to the dictionary:
and you get stuck on a random word *shofar*

which is *a ram's horn blown as a wind instrument,*
sounded in Biblical times chiefly
to communicate signals in battle
and announce certain religious occasions,
and you wonder why everything is turning up
rams and goats and other horned animals here lately.

You shake it off and get back to snag:
n. *a tree or part of a tree held fast*
in the bottom of a river or other body
of water and forming an impediment
or danger to navigation. So, yes,

you spelled it right, but the fact remains
that snag is not a good thing, because
even though you know *Urban Dictionary*
will say something slick about sex,
or possibly sausages, snag is still

n. *any obstacle or impediment*
and v.i. *to become entangled*
with some obstacle or hindrance.
While becoming entangled with someone is
enticing, I've had enough of the obstacles,

thank you. You won't find me in the shallows,
a reed straw in my mouth, waiting for a man
as river grass, limbs, fish bloated and fish full of holes,
the collar of a lost dog, the jaw bone of a god lost,
muster to my horns, twisted instruments.
My own magnificent impediments.

Geography

If time is a dimension   like space

       Los Angeles exists   Dublin exists

then you and I spark   you and I laugh
in North Carolina   at a dive bar in Georgia
over a few beers   over a line of salted shots.

       You unpin my hair
                               unpin

unpin

A king-sized hotel bed in Charleston,
white cotton sheets across my bare back,
the space next to me untouched.

       Cairo   Santa Fe

                           I run my fingers over white. Feel
                           the hollow from your hip,
                           indentation on the pillow in

     another bed where you face me (Miami)
             shuddered breath between bated lips (Meridian).

Poem Automatic

The anagram maker takes the letters of my name,
throws them up in the one and zero-littered
space occupying tiny etched lines of gold like Nazca
drawings meaning something to someone far,
far above. And looking down from the mother-
ship, zips out 93,751 combinations beginning
with A Referable Mingle which is auto-brilliant.
People immediately mingle at a bar in Blacksburg,
cigarettes held in the air as they travel along courses
created by bodies and visible from gel lights focused
on the stage as crossing trails of smoke. I refer
to it. It was before I could interpret tracings
you shivered on my back, before your hands pressed
into me so deep, I could not live long enough,
shed enough skin, erode enough. That even though
those letters also spell Ameba Genre Filler,
Alarming Beef Leer, I keep coming back
to Blacksburg. Our bodies pressed tight
in the crowd. My only signs fingers fretting
chords and cords vibrating together creating
a song about a once-met-girl who made such
an impression. I keep coming back to you.

Recollections

Kareem Abdul-Jabbar lost his jazz collection
in a house fire in 1983, somewhere around
3,000 albums. Everyone in the universe
followed the Lakers back then. I remember
watching his hands flip that gorgeous balletic skyhook
swish. Kareem's teammates tried to replace
some of the albums, as records are replaceable.
And so are books. But replacements
are never the records with the carefully-handled
covers and pored-over liner notes. Never
the same 33 1/3 so well-played you could drop
the needle exactly at the beginning
of that song. You know the one. Never the same
book you gifted me with hands I can't
forget. I read the whole thing, you know,
in my car that night in 1983
after watching the game with you. After
watching the game with you, there was fire.
And then, just like that, you were gone.

3-5 Days without Water

The human body is 60% water.
Cry me a river.
It is often recommended that humans drink 64oz. of water per day.
Alice cried herself a pool and floated right through the keyhole
searching for the white rabbit.
71% of the earth is covered in water.
My mother kept a Mason jar for our tears next to the vitamins
in the high cabinet.
Your face flooded with tears.
Your eyes are limpid pools. I drown in them.
On shore, there is a mouse, a duck, a dodo. They cannot get dry,
and the sea is high and counting.
I feel your pull.
It is all very confusing.
Tears always make me think of Alice and glass jars.
And things that make me small.
I want you to wash over me like the tide.
I burn to drink you in.

Listening to Hendrix on vinyl, eating breakfast, and thinking of your hands

Life is an LP record, a vinyl disk pressed in a continuous spiral,
moving inward from a vast expanse to a tight circle of bright black
where the music ends.
If you start at my left big toe, you can unpeel my skin in one, long,
curvy strip like the devil peels a hard-boiled egg.
Skin like the salted soft white dome, teeth through thick yolk.
Thin skin, just a cover, a network of cells. When pressed, it sounds
like a diamond-tipped needle in a v-shaped groove. Gently drop the arm.
Jimi Hendrix live grinds the span of my hips, slides around my ribs.
My skin can no more be removed than the devil from your hand.
I don't believe in the devil.
An egg's thin skin is a cold blue when held to the light,
membrane less like a shroud and more like a sliding glass door.
Pull it aside. Step through.

Dear Valentine,

I(t) probably   wouldn't have worked
anyway. You like runny eggs and think it's
funny to pretend nothing is
unusual here. Your ex-wife's name is
Joy, and I can(t) compete with   love
poems, rainbows, lascivious conduct.
My hands are clammy and you   shuck
oysters. My breath is shallow and
you throw a bait net like a comma   catch
me in a moment of   beer and black
dresses, silver anchors, backless pause
backed into. A moment inappropriate
for happiness   spite of clean shirts and
belted slacks. Nose to chest, hear(t) words
like do you still feel   sweet
         roses are just roses. What would you
have me?   or where. Despite our
no(t)   never let you.   Go.

Your Mask Is a Gift

Let's meet tonight. I'll be Wonder
Woman, & you can wear your Batman mask.
I'll take the rocker with the broken
slat if you take the one missing
an arm. Gift me with story, & I will gift
you with wine. Let's drink until our hearts

forget we've been apart, forget that hearts
are just two-fisted vessels of muscle, wondrous
pumps. I will raise strong arms, turn, display my gift
for spontaneous costume change. Your mask
will not quite hide your eyes; I have missed
them. Without you, I have been broken.

It's cliché, but each time we part, I break
a little more. My big, powerful heart
grips the empty space where you are missing
& drinks it in. I'll lasso you & wonder
how I'll let go. If I'll be able to mask
the truth. Tell me the one about the gift

of a dark night, of the stolen gift
of stars, of conversation broken
only by the crime of sunrise when our masks
fell back into place. When my heart
clenched like a fist. I will wonder
at the texture of your cape, at your belt missing

bolas & batarangs. Proof that I miss
most of your life. We will drink to the gift
of time. I'll tell you the one about the wonder
of life breathed into clay, of that which was broken.
You'll tell me the one about hearts
and distance, about necessary masks.

Let's meet tonight. Let's drop our requisite masks.
Let's fly away. Let's go missing.
Let's listen close as our fisted hearts
beat open. Let's drink deep and gift
each other with nothing less than broken
roles & a shared sense of wonder.

Tonight, I greet your mask as a gift
because missing you unmasked breaks
my heart. My wonderful, fist-fighting heart.

Love with No Apparent Function

Junk DNA, long senseless stretches
of the twisted ladder corresponding,
apparently, to nothing. Perhaps
that is where you lie.

Like farmers plowing fields where entire
civilizations have flourished and crumbled,
turning up chunks of seeming stone, carved curve
of cheek, of buttock buried in dirt meant
to be seeded. Ancient art banished
for its offense to the conquering horde.
Artifacts levered out of fertile ground
into the measured foundation of a barn,
layered and lathered in rough mortar.
The part that is often overlooked.

I would ride haggard through your field, furrowed,
for the chance find in the considered seam,
the pearl in the inspired incision,
the tongued chalice lip of chisel,
the hammered rigid edge. I would kneel
before your ballast-built base to find
where you enter me.

I would blister my palms with climbing, grip
the rough-cut rungs composed of waste, shake
sieved in my savaged throat. Salvage fire.

You can skip this part.
You put your evolving tongue everywhere.

Devenir Chêvre

to be driven mad is
to become a goat, head down
butting, rearing up
on tiny hind hooves.

you are driving me mad.
my temples throb budding
bone, keratin. my horns
are coming out heavy.

this is driving me mad.
my shoulders and neck ache
with its weight. I should
give up. but I bow up,

shoulders squared in tense
attitude, head down.

boire comme un trou
to drink like a hole is

to be driven mad is
to become a goat, head down.
I refuse to yield. I drink, I fall
deep. this is not a failure.

to drink like a hole is
to fall. to fall is to see
up, up from the bottom, up
from where pasture light trips,

traps on temporary rocks,
slick as fire and just as dark.
I fall to become a goat
I must not fail to be.

Sex with a Novelist

Make your lover want
something. A glass of water.
A plane ticket to Tucson.
A vein full of heroin.
A puppy. Great sex. Don't
give it to her.

The Happily Married Woman Boards the Plane

Please don't be witty as hell sitting in the window seat on a six-hour flight with a two-hour delay on the tarmac, and don't tell stories that make me snort and say oh you're cute without being condescending, and don't look even remotely like Viggo Mortensen or Christian Bale in the *Dark Knight* but not *American Psycho*, 'cause that's creepy. Although I'd prefer creepy on this flight over spending twenty minutes of shushing, tearing-up laughter quoting *The Holy Grail* and *LOTR*, precious, and seriously, if you know what *LOTR* stands for and you say Samwise Gamgee is your favorite character, I'll ask to change seats. Please be dumb as a bag of hammers. Please don't order Maker's Mark and ask if I'd care for one, too, and then toast to new friends and clink the little bottles and say "clink" and wink at me. Please be wearing sandals and have cracked, yellow toenails, or at the very least please be wearing tennis shoes without socks, or boat shoes without socks. 'Cause then I won't feel like I'm missing something when I pop my earbuds in and start to read the opening to *The Gunslinger*, again. And if I do, don't be polite and let me read and when I get up to use the restroom and come back say, "The man in black fled across the desert, and the gunslinger followed." Best line in literature. Or if you do, at least have the courtesy to have obviously profuse body hair, like eyebrows an inch long, visible curly ear hair, back hair flowing across the collar of your *Yo Gabba Gabba*! t-shirt. At the very least, have a fit when the stewardess forgets your second bourbon. Don't you dare say, it's ok, sugar. Would you bring two, pretty please? We're celebrating the discovery of distillation, and then start a conversation on the philosophy behind the end of the *Dark Tower* series, ancient alien theory, or Rushdie's take on hybridity. And god, if you do, throw me a line and, for no apparent reason, say you hate cats, hate your roommates, hate your wife. Or, just say you love your wife and be done with it. Because no matter what the love songs say, I know in six or fifteen years, you'd leave your running shoes on the table one more time, your wet towel on the floor; you'd drink the last Diet Coke, eat the very last piece of sourdough bread, and leave me the heel.

T & A

I know I'm not supposed to notice
how the pictures on the table of contents
in my Williams-Sonoma soup book all
resemble breasts. Yellow onions fat

at one end, narrow at the other,
cremini mushrooms flattish with small domes,
tomato globes, beets, even scattered garlic
cloves, small and pointy. I'll admit, I've caught

myself doing the down & up,
appreciating a woman's form,
mentally slapping myself for looking.
And even if you're not a breast person

there's the ass, which on either sex
can make you feel as though you have no control
over your own eyes, the windows to your
soul or your libido, whichever arrives

first. And why does it become so difficult?
Remember when you could say, I like you,
you're pretty and nice, without sounding
like a perv, without insulting someone's

gender, without it being taken as
I'd really like to fuck you, may I please?
I guess we can't have that back. It's childish.
But I'm looking through this book of soups

and I find mussels *mariniere*, dark halves parting
to reveal slick flesh, small skin straining
at the whorled base, ingredients
much more appealing than the finished

product. Visceral in their natural
state. I know I'm not supposed to look.
I know I'm not supposed to like it
when a man's eyes say what our culture

won't let him speak without a lawsuit.
I know that tits & ass are off the table,
that I shouldn't think about them being
on a table amongst other fruit-

and-vegetable-like parts, that sometimes
zucchini is just zucchini, and scanning
a man's parcel is definitely out.
I know that I don't want to be an object

any more than I want to be a pair
of blushing cherries, that my husband knows
to say *I'd like to lick your brain* while he cups
my butt in a well-fitting pair of jeans,

my breasts under a tight tangerine tee.
But, as much as I hate to admit it,
my brain is often rebellious, caring
less for the practical value

of pears, of plums, of penetrating
bees, than for the way that breasts and behinds
remind me: luscious body, what a gift
to revel in your physical feast.

Glamour Church

I attend the stained-glass panels on your back.
I buck faith. The bold cobalt of the sea
swirls the bowl of your hips, the cold gray
waterspout column snakes your spine.
I hear the spell spun, the roar. Glitter-scaled
water dragon circles your ribs, teeth
at your shoulder, whiskers trail to your neck,
your slippery side. Your jeweled eyes draw
lightning. There is truth in rain. I trace
the black outline of electric claws,
hear them scrabble on wet rocks. Push faith.
I kneel at your feet, attend the scroll writ
on tender flesh. My unleashed hair brushes
your ocean-damp skin. I have no faith
in paper. You have glamoured me. I attend.

Mooning

My lover's rear is nothing like the moon,
especially when framed in chrome, speeding
along the 95 at 80 miles per hour
just because Jesus Saves was plastered
across the aerodynamic expense
of the Benz in the fast lane. The Truth
Jesus fish eating Darwin didn't help
matters much. She climbed into the back
seat, hung her highly evolved behind out
the left window, screamed Catch up to him!
And I did, just like anything.
                              Because
she still believes that moonbathing cancels
out a burn, and when we climb to the tarred roof,
gravel biting into the soft, pale soles
of our feet, her shoulder skin silvers,
flashes like minnows at the river's edge,
like a sinuous baby blacktip shark
skirting flaxen sand. I am at once
charmed and caught in the gut. *La luna* etches
grainy hollows in her face. She will not
be held, I know. I can only follow
her phases, watch stars fall around her. Lift
my eyes to her unapproachable light.

Pedestal

I am compelled to think of you
as golden Colossus
astride the bay,
legs planted deep
in salt and murky bottom.

But then, that whole idea of the huge statue of Helios,
bronze reflecting the Mediterranean sun, sending its light
back across the dome of sky like a streamlined chariot,
as standing with one enormous leg on one side
and one on the other is wrong, isn't it? Sailed beneath
the giant pendant phallus did no ship ever.
And besides, the sheer dead-weight of the bronze
would have toppled his great crowned head right into the deep.

At any rate, Colossus fell, and people went to see the pieces.
Imagine the selfies! Here's me with my arms not quite reaching
around the sun god's left big toe. Kids climbing up on monstrous feet,
posing at the jagged ends of marble ankles. It's a popular metaphor,
seeing the great ones fall. Liberty's patina-ed head regularly lolls
in big-screen water off the coast of New York, as anyone raised
to such heights seems to inevitably fall, kicking up silt.

But I think of you this way anyway,
your bright corona blinding my eyes
held ever up.

Murmuration

Massive turning and twisting.
Moving as one is
suspended reality.
Uncanny coordination,
beautifully known.
Systems poised to tip,
to be transformed.
Metals magnetized, liquids turning
to gas. Each is connected
to every other.
The rules are relatively simple:
When a [lover] moves,
so do you.

Sourced from: Keim, Brandon. "The Startling Science of a Starling Murmuration." *Wired.* 8 November 2011. Web. 15 November 2015.

All The Things We Have In Common

1. We are both standing on paddleboards.
2. We are both wishing we were someplace else.
3. We are both thinking that the clouds reflected in the river below us look like breasts
4. because someone is playing "Girls, Girls, Girls" really loud from their boat
5. and we are both thinking about strip clubs.
6. We were both teenagers in the '80s and played the shit out of that album.
7. We both still think Nikki Sixx is hot.
8. We are both thinking that the clouds reflected in the river below us look like breasts
9. because we are both replaying that one night in our heads
10. and we are both thinking about someone else.
11. We are both standing on paddleboards
12. on a river where we have both stripped down
13. shot our bodies through clouds reflected like breasts
14. stood, bare skin dripping, sky rippling out on the mirror surface
15. and thought about that one night in the '80s
16. when we were both someplace else with someone else
17. and we are both wishing.
18. We are both standing on paddleboards.
19. We are both playing air guitar and screaming "Girls, girls, girls!"
20. and thinking how much we have in common.

How Things Build: On Botticelli's *Primavera*

According to Ovid, Chloris is Flora after the rape.
Zephyrus makes her his wife, and she's ok with that.
I'm not so sure. In *Primavera*, Chloris is sand,
and the West Wind is gray-green, the color of stone,
the color of nothing. Zero as tempest, marking
its place. Bougainvillea births paper blooms in her mouth,
a baby in her belly. I am reminded of a story

about a lazy boy who fell asleep beneath
a tree when he was supposed to be working. A bird
dropped a seed which fell directly into lazy boy's
nose. He was so lazy, and he slept for so long
that the seed grew into a tree. Zero plus one equals
one. I imagine the roots curling down his wet throat,
working through his body's water until his skin

peels off like birch bark, his ribs scatter like so many
dead Isabelline branches blown down by a strong
wind. His jaw separates and falls to moss-covered
earth where it is found, years later, at the base
of a great tree, gnarled roots the color of bougainvillea.
It is picked up by a woman made of sand. With it
she slays a thousand men. As they fall, their blood vines
her skin, and from her mouth, a galaxy of blooms.

Cross Streets

Black asphalt ripples in the midday heat.
Hardened soles of my feet resist the burn,
skip towards the corner where Compton meets
my block. Concrete sidewalks pass the totem
woman, her black hair strung across her face.
Her gnarled hands clutch a worn brown paper bag
like a wayward child. This dying place,
asylum on the boulevard, a jag
in my throat. Heat reddens my cheeks as I try
not to look, not to stare at her standing
like dark Venus in a housecoat. Blackening sky,
the ozone snap of the streetlight coming
on. Time for home. My tongue, like leather, chokes.
The slap of feet quickens; this street my yoke.

The slap of feet quickens; this street my yoke.
Carlos was beautiful scaling the wall,
vaulting my balcony and laughing, smoke
circling his thick black braid. His siren call
pulled me to the cliff; whalesong and speed:
now he dances me down evening-cooled asphalt
to Sunken City. Edge of real; tectonic need
for subduction collides us, wet with salt
spray and sweat. The ocean reclaims us,
and the stars here are bright, blown clean and clear.
His profile is tight. A compressed spring must
release its energy, spiraling out. Fear
licks my edges; his fingertips burn,
spiral galaxies' stars die young, and yearn.

Spiral galaxies' stars die young, and yearn,
in their little deaths, for reincarnation.
Jay dances a mean two-step. He leads; I learn
to slide the leather of my boots. Friction
creates heat, and I smell his skin, sweat-damp
curling small hairs at the base of his skull.
His fingertips press the small of my back; I tamp

down the fire and quick, quick, slow, slow. His pull
spins me in and close; across my chest, tightens
his arm, a moment, and releases me.
We circle the wooden floor. The lights brighten;
the music fades. On the freeway home, he
asks again. I shake my head, ignore the sparks,
dervishes whirling in the ecstatic dark.

Dervishes whirling in the ecstatic dark:
the prismatic haloes circling streetlights
seen through my chlorine bloodshot eyes. The bark
of tires on asphalt rends the desert night.
Mike beside me in the VW
croons his part. Tony to my Maria.
He is gay, I know, but my skin still sings,
shivers. Mike's boys' choir tenor aria
fills the van, slips out the open window;
my breath quickens as he runs long fingers
over the cracked dash, playing out the slow
minor chord lament. Maria lingers.
Mike leans on the strip of chrome, his face framed
in metal and night. He sings for me a name.

In metal and night, Oscar sings my name,
the Spanish version, with a lilting "a"
at the end. Then, the French, a breathy game
of vowels and innuendo. "*Non.*" "*Mais,
oui.*" "*Mais non*, Oscar." "*Mais oui*, Gabrielle."
The English "yes" too serious to utter
off stage. On the road to Kingsville, he tells
me about his ex. Lonely, he putters
around their house. He eats over the sink.
The drive from Corpus Christi lays the body
bare; black Texas night, miles of flat-black ink.
My house is dark. The streetlights seem gaudy,
spotlighting our foreheads together, still
lips, once electric under hot gels.

Electric pink lips under hot stage gels,
a tiny bar off-strip in Myrtle Beach.
My girlfriend dances with Dave who later tells
her he's relieved 'cause they have two kids each.
Dads have trouble meeting women. Dave's friend,
my surprise; yet another not-to-be.
We talk Vonnegut, society's end,
the "everyone makes the team" mentality,
Dostoevsky's underground man who might,
but never does, how Prufrock's impotence
trumps free will. What good are these moments, these bright
meetings? Tantalizing torture, my "good sense"
keeps me just out of reach. Against the posts,
I beat my fists, recall these many ghosts.

The totem woman balls her fist. Her ghost
straps me with silence, flays my restrained skin
until the layers speak. Red muscle boasts
strength, bone solidity. I am her kin,
not her kind. I move street to street to street.
Test their lines, their curves, their intersections.
Taste the grit of the empty fields, the run
of the stream behind the mill, the junction
of desert sky and blacktop. The woman's hair,
strung across her face. She clutches the brown
paper bag. I am no wayward child. Dare
me. Until they are not, the cross streets own
us. I lie down with the road, cheek to cheek.
Black asphalt ripples in the midday heat.

In all the months that end

I often obsess about the walrus and the carpenter,
the bed of oyster babies, their blankets pink and blue
tucked around their fat fat bodies and into the edges
of their luminous shells. Their little shoes like beans
carrying them quick across assassin sand.

What if the carpenter had been a butterfly
or a baronet? An elephant or editor? A prisoner
or poetess? Syllables trip across the page and rip
meat from shell with the blunt edge of an heirloom
pocket-knife. The walrus can keep his handkerchief.

I will not hide my face behind a slip of whisker,
a trap of stabbing tusk. I will not speak of ships
sailing quick across smoky harbors, bearing messages
sealed in colored wax to kings. I will stand at water's edge,
salt dripping from my quivering chin, and I will eat.

Thanks and love to Denise Duhamel and Suzanne Cleary for teaching me to be brave in my writing by being brave in their own, and for reminding me that poetry can be fun (and funny!). To R.T. Smith for his guidance on revision. To all the poets and writers I've met over the past six years for loving this art, and especially to the MFA faculty and students at Converse for all their encouragement and support. To Kathleen Nalley for helping me keep my priorities straight. And to my mom for being creative and for teaching me to be creative, too.

GBF

Gabrielle Brant Freeman's poetry has been published in many journals, including *Barrelhouse, Hobart, Melancholy Hyperbole, Rappahannock Review, Shenandoah, storySouth*, and *Waxwing*. She was nominated twice for the *Best of the Net*, and she was a 2014 finalist. Freeman won the 2015 Randall Jarrell Poetry Competition, and she received a Regional Artist Grant in 2015 from the North Carolina Arts Council. Freeman earned her MFA through Converse College. This is her first book of poetry.

Cover artist Dawn D. Surratt studied art at the University of North Carolina at Greensboro as a recipient of the Spencer Love Scholarship in Fine Art. She has exhibited her work throughout the Southeast and currently works as a freelance designer and artist. Her work has been published internationally in magazines, on book covers, and in print media. She lives on the beautiful Kerr Lake in northern North Carolina with her husband, one demanding cat, and a crazy Pembroke Welsh Corgi.

www.ingramcontent.com/pod-product-compliance
Lightning Source LLC
LaVergne TN
LVHW041345080426
835512LV00006B/630